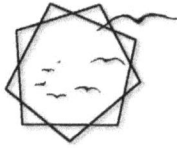

Muse

with

Blue
Apples

Muse

with

Blue
Apples

ANTHOLOGY OF THE
NEW MEXICO POETRY ALLIANCE

Blue Muse with Apples
Anthology of the New Mexico Poetry Alliance
Copyright ©2016 New Mexico Poetry Alliance

Managing Editor: Karin Stangl

ISBN: 978-1-940769-50-9
Publisher: Mercury HeartLink
Printed in the United States of America

Cover image: digital adaptation
of "Frau mit Äpflen" by August Macke

Contact Karin Stangl, editor:
mariposa_verde@q.com

Mercury HeartLink
www.heartlink.com

Muse with Blue Apples

OLGA ANSON

CLARA ANN BOWLER

TRISH CLAFLIN

DON DeNOON

KATHY MAXSON

KAREN MCKINNON

RAYMOND MOCK

BEN NURRY

MARTY O'MALLEY

Karin Stangl

Acknowledgments

Don DeNoon's poem, "Checking Out," was published in *Fixed and Free Poetry Anthology*, 2015.

Karen McKinnon's poem, "A Winter's Wake: Song for the Solstice," was published in *Coming True* by Watermelon Mountain Press, 2000.

Thanks to Jeanne Favret, Joann Sheets, and Karin Stangl for their work in compiling this anthology of poems by members of the New Mexico Poetry Alliance.

This book is dedicated to poets
Constance Hester and B.J. Skinner, who
were sterling in their commitment to their
wordsmithing craft. They were beloved
members of New Mexico Poetry Alliance
for many years. Both passed on in 2014.

We cherish their respective contributions
to this group.

MUSE WITH BLUE APPLES

Seductive muse beckons
From a silver, misted pool.

Come closer
To water's edge, poet.
Be lulled by cricket song
And fragrant flowers wafting.
Discard the sandals,
And dip your toes
Into cool, layered stillness.
Stir the reflected moon to life.
Create a ripple of words
That merge together
Into harmonic ecstasy.

Follow her and be immersed,
Weightless and buoyant.
As a rhythmic flow begins,
Capture that mystical essence in a small jar.
Baptized in your craft, emerge
Satisfied and nourished.
Lie down
In green grass

Robe falls in random folds,
Damp, cool, and refreshed.

Bite into one of the crisp blue apples
The muse placed in your pocket,
As a parting gift
With a promise to return.

—*Karin Stangl*

Do What You Love

Purgatory is real they told me.
Is it the same as being in limbo?
I thought the limbo was a dance.
Neither here, nor there, living without purpose
Just waiting in line to get into heaven.
Like an amber traffic signal
Waiting to be told, to stop or go.

Like being engaged thirty three years.
Purgatory, is it a place or just a state of being?
Love flows sweetly and purely when it is new.
"It's always good at the beginning."
How does one keep it flowing?
I wish I knew.

A lady in waiting,
Neither here, nor there.
Just waiting for the day I could do what I really loved to do
Time slipped away.
Sciatica, plantar fasciitis, osteoporosis,
It's not so easy now to kneel and plant a garden.

THE PASSING OF...

They say divorce is like death
The death of a marriage and all that it stood for
Thoughts, memories, and possessions left behind
Dreams, hopes, the love
All of it gone
No more to be seen or felt

Gone slowly as one might go in a slow and agonizing illness
Gone swiftly not knowing how, when or why
Was it an accident?
Gone forever, ever so final, so hopeless, so helpless, so sorry
Not a day goes by that I don't miss you
Not a day passes without a tear
Yes, it's true
Divorce is like death

TAKE TWO: TRANSFORMATION

A great and mighty Sphinx stares across the desert
The developer swells with pride
Sagebrush, eucalyptus fragrance of the rain kissed desert
Mesas transformed into planned communities
With houses and parks

Waxing moon over desecrated volcanic cones
Spotlight on coyote shadows howling
Must the roadrunner now live in the asphalt city?
The cuckoo jumps from wall to street
His feet race over beds of red hot coals

Quail nest in sagebrush
Where do they go?
The answer, unsympathetic, and merciless as the sun
The developer swells with pride
A great and mighty Sphinx stares across the desert.

HYPNOTIC RECALL

Should I forget you? Forget that you were ever
A part of my life.
That even for one split second you ever
Looked into my eyes,
Held my hand, touched my soul, stole my heart?

Should I forget you? Like the tiny sea shell cast
Upon the sands of the shore,
Seen but for a millisecond through the clouded waters.
Anxiously I reached out to pick up the beautiful shell,
Just within the reach of my grasp.

As I opened my hand,
My heart stopped in breathless anticipation of
The beautiful treasure of the sea, that I might
Hold in my hand to gaze upon.

But instead of the exquisite treasure, I had so hoped
To find therein,
The receding waves had washed it away,
Through my fingers,
Leaving only small finely polished pebbles behind.

Stones, handsome in their own right,
But not the lovely little shell
I had in an instant so impetuously set my heart upon.

Ah! I know, 'tis foolish
To overlook the beauty of the others
That would so gladly nestle in the palm of my hand,
All for the want of that one little shell.

Yet, it was washed by the waters,
Back into the eternal womb of the sea.
Never again to be seen by me,

To be washed ashore,
Perhaps some other time, perhaps no other time
For another's eye to see,
Hand to hold, soul to touch, heart to love

And my heart began to beat again,
For it knew, though the intellect and emotions
Be slow to accept it,
That I must go on, on to pick other shells,
Which might also escape my reach,

Leaving only the small, finely polished stones behind
Until, finally, I might actually come
To prefer their allurement.
Shells break so easily, you know.
(Rocks have more inside, you know).

The Color Blue

The first rose bush I ever planted
was a blue rose.
The nursery man said
I was his first customer of the year.
Translated: "You have to be crazy
to plant a bare-root rose bush
in January in Albuquerque."
My scraggly bush
prospered and merged
with a hybrid white.
So, the blossoms are really light purple,
but they bloom on a single cane
with the white hybrids
if you don't look too closely
at the interlocking stems.
A multi-colored rose bush
from a colored illustration
in "Alice in Wonderland."
For thirty-five years,
my blue rose has never faded –
Unlike my blue eyes
which have turned to grey.
Unlike the blue sky
which hides behind
a dust storm.
Unlike my daughter's quilt
which barely survived a tentative trip
through the washing machine.
Unlike the shaggy blue carpeting
I ordered for the basement floor
when we moved our master bedroom
below grade to avoid the stairs.

MY MUSE

My muse sits in bed with me at night
as I toss, turn and roll,
trying to make sense of today's events.
She used to dictate eloquent introductions
which turned the heads of judges
in support of legal clients.
She reminded me of hidden evidence,
and recited arguments
on why an off-hand comment
by a district judge in Montana
was greater than a learned opinion
by the New York Court of Appeals.
Without her, my legal briefs
would have been empty clichés
downloaded from the Internet.
In retirement, my bedside muse
has turned to more important matters,
like gardens and birds,
and close family members.
She introduces me to fantasy characters
who mumble sideways comments
on politics and current events.
She comforts me
with satire and sarcasm,
when life's experiences
are more than I can bear.
Then, with a wink and a grin,
she disappears into the ventilation system,
leaving me alone in the fear and chaos
of my early morning dreams.

APPLE PIE

"She can make an apple pie,
quick as a cat can wink an eye."

The old gal takes longer:
An hour and a half to peel and core the apples.
A half an hour to chill the pie dough.
Another quarter hour to mix the sugar and cinnamon filling,
to slice the apples and heat the oven.
A quarter hour, at least, to assemble
the bottom crust, the apples and filling,
twenty minutes to lay out the latticed top crust on the pie.
Everyone knows it takes
ten minutes at high heat
to brown the lattice crust
and thirty minutes at medium heat
to bake the apples and filling.
Not to mention the thirty–one years
of tender care in cultivating
a McIntosh apple tree
in an irrigated Albuquerque backyard.
Orchards are delicate in the high country:
An early spring sprouts tender blossoms.
A late frost kills the flowers before the fruit matures.
The old lady lacks a pruning hook or chemical bug spray.
Her fruit is dwarfed and full of rot.
This is my second pie of the season.
I am not going to obsess over details.

PLANET PLUTO'S HEART

I saw a heart–shaped light on Pluto.
Rounded shoulders, triangular torso,
ending in a shadowed point,
Direct to me from outer space.
Photographed by the New Horizons spacecraft
during a brief fly–by.
Transmitted three billion miles to a space laboratory
where it was downloaded into a video.
Transmitted again to the public broadcasting system
where it was re–edited and packed into my TV cable.
Carried by the cable to my TV,
which scanned the pixels
at the best speed for human recognition.
Light from my high–definition TV,
filtered through my cataracts,
molded in a familiar form
by the memories and fantasies
in my damaged temporal lobe.
My personal valentine
from the dwarf planet
at the edge of the solar system,
visible only to me.
Healthier visions and better equipment at the space lab
will enable the scientists to argue
whether Pluto's tall mountains of ice
arise from a solid frozen sphere,
or the crust over a hot core
where Plutonian single–cell life forms
are slowly evolving.

But three billion miles
and all the illusions
prevent them from proving
that Pluto never had a heart.

BOXES

I've put the past
In boxes
Big boxes, little boxes.
Some are sealed
Up tight
Put away in an attic
Never to be opened.
There's more than a few

Of them.

Other boxes
Are with me always.
I bring them with me
From home to home
Open them one at a time
When I want
To remember.

As I untie
The pretty ribbons
Lift the lids
To inhale the fragrance
Of dried flowers
And touch faded photographs
The memories are sweet

SWAMP THING

Back in the bayou
Lived a woman
Don't you know
Few had ever seen her
She was called Marie Laveau

Now Marie brewed a potion
That would cause strange emotions
She could charm you
Don't you know
Get you in her power
When the moon was hanging low

She'd dance
Fandangos to Santana
Feed you
Mangos and bananas
Till you'd
Do just what
She wanted
Don't you know

Then you'd love
The witchy woman
With her voodoo and her frog
Help her draw her pentagrams
And howl together in the fog

Folks would wonder what happened
To that man who disappeared
Was he lost in the swamp
As everybody feared?

Guess the gators got him.

Fireflies

Glowing incandescent
Phosphorescent light
Caught in the hand
They are cool
The feathery tickle
Of tiny wings
And a faint glow
Between the fingers

Hold them gently
Release them
To the night
Watch them flash
Their code of love
Like fallen stars
Pulsing their energy
In the dance of life.

MANATEE DREAMS

From crystal waters
Bubbling up
From deep beneath the ground
Where limestone rivers flow

There the lazy manatee
Sleeps away the winter days
Drifting in the warmth
Of spring–fed streams.

And rises to the surface
To breathe without wakening
From green dreams
Of juicy water hyacinths.

Its round, smooth body
Moving so slowly
Among the waving strands
Of supple eel grass.

Gently floating
Above white sands
Like a great gray cloud
The manatee dreams.

Checking Out

They first saw each other in the pickle aisle
Elbows bumped as they reached for different jars
He selected dills, she sweet baby gherkins
He smiled, excused his clumsiness
She was rendered speechless by his soft blue eyes
He waited until she moved her cart
Then he steered down another aisle

Their carts met again at Aisle Six—pasta sauces
He gallantly gestured for her to go first
She wilted inside but bravely asked
Do you prefer Ragú or Prego?
He pointed to Newman's Own and placed a jar in his cart
She followed his lead.
Again they parted.

At Checkout she arrived first
He moved his cart in line behind her and asked her name
Jill. Jill Anderson
I'm Larry. Larry Mills and quickly added
I hope our elbows bump into each other again sometime soon
She smiled, paid her bill and retrieved a card from her wallet
Placing it in his palm she invited, *Call me.*

PRAYER IN THE STREETS OF BAGHDAD

Robert
Protected in battle
Helmet and body armor
Rifle and ammo
Trained to kill
Patrolling streets of Baghdad

Ahmed
Engaged in battle
No armor, no helmet
No rifle, but an I.E.D.
Trained to kill
Hiding in streets of Baghdad

Explosion
Severs limbs
Firefight erupts
Insurgent flees
Soldier aims rifle
Ahmed falls on street in Baghdad

Medic comforts
Robert holds crucifix
Prays *Hail Mary*
Ahmed clutches Quran
Proclaims *Allah is great*
While God weeps over streets of Baghdad

COMMON MEAL

My body was not hungry
But still I ate
My flesh was not thirsty
And yet I drank

My soul it was that hungered
And my spirit was athirst
So I ate the bread
And drank the wine
To satisfy a longing
Deep within

QUESTIONS

How far does a snowflake fall
To touch a child's outstretched tongue?

How high must a fever rise
Before a sense of wellness is restored?

How many fits of anger must be endured
Before harmony is achieved?

How many rainbows does it take
To show a storm has passed?

How deeply does one person need to feel another's pain
Before the two are united by grace?

How far does one need to travel
To reach a place called Wisdom?

How long does a life need to be
Before a soul makes its journey home?

How wide does a break in the clouds need to be
To allow a soul into heaven?

LET'S MAKE A DEAL

Citizen Deb enters a Washington, D.C. hotel tavern
While a large, tall man and a tall, blonde woman
In casual clothes talk loudly.
Citizen Deb sits in a corner and waits for her food and tea
As these friends keep talking business.
Citizen Deb writes a postcard to her mom
About her visit to the Library of Congress.
Then the friends talk about their rich Chinese friends.
The blonde brags about her trip to Dubai
And how she gave a talk in the Bay area.
She even circled the globe twice in twenty days!
Next she promises to carry a bill for her lobbyist friend.
Citizen Deb never hears such words as:
"Thank you for bringing this crucial national issue
To my attention."
Nor does she hear:
"This is an issue my constituents hold dear."
The lobbyist throws his weight around
On his way to the hotel lobby and
The blond follows with powerful strides
In her expensive boots.
Citizen Deb will never know how the deal was sealed.

THE FLUTE SPEAKS

Two hours ago I began with a yoga of scales,
Allowing my master to warm breath and muscles.
In harmony we worshipped and prayed.
Next we saluted the flag with Francis Scott Key,

    Waltzed with Strauss,
    Marched with Sousa,
    Frolicked with Mozart,
    Rhapsodized with Faure,
    Skipped to childhood songs,
    And traveled the world through folk songs.

Then we slipped into a meditative
Stanza of "Amazing Grace,"
Crescendoed to a jubilant climax.
We are ready to perform for anyone, anywhere.

Hand Me Downs

Hand–me–down clothes should be called something else
Like, "Please don't do without"
"Let me help you out"
Or better yet
"Love passed onward and upward the human chain"
Or simply
"Love shares"

THE JOY OF VISUAL ARTS AND MUSIC

A juried arts and crafts fair awakens my creative spirit
Through many colors, textures and forms.
I delight in the masterfully decorated silk lamp shades
of the featured artist.
Singers playing guitar fill the air with familiar music.
One jewelry maker welcomes me to her listserv after
the purchase of subtly luminescent earrings.
A glass maker and her husband take extra care with
a purchase of a small, square plate.
A teenage girl, in need of money to pay
for a lost school book,
sells me a faux dinosaur egg as a child's gift item.
Joyfully I discover sheer nylon flowers and flowers
made of sheet music.
A former supervisor of mine, now a painter graciously
welcomes me to her booth of New Mexico landscapes.
Now a slender bouquet of sheer calla lilies
grace my living room.
All in all, I am enthralled by this date with my husband.

REASSURANCE IN AUTUMN NIGHT SKIES

We are separate sparks—
Fires near each other,
Camping neighbors.

We need others to gather
Kindling, sticks, logs and
Tend our fires through late night hours.

Seeing your porch light on,
I turn mine on, too.
Homing neighbors.

We will sleep soon.
Jupiter and Venus, so bright,
Travel the night sky.

Even though
I know these things,
I reach out to touch your voice.

I AM THINKING

I am thinking of a Cymbidium orchid
The purple and green stalk
is moved to the corner office
to get more light each weekend.

I am thinking of a wandering Jew.
The purple and green plant
is permitted to go to the Orient
where Hasidic rabbi listens to haiku.

I am thinking of a former Geisha girl.
The purple and green kimono
is permitted to be unpacked
as the gazing man asks her to twirl.

I am thinking of a Samurai warrior.
The purple and green helmet
is permitted to be worn by his children
and the gentle man is no longer a destroyer.

PERFUME BUS

Elderly women, (the widows),
are sitting on the perfume bus
waiting. Prisoner like, they
longingly look at their
corner of the morning sky.
They wait to go to the some place:

Some place where their face is sacred.
Some place where they can watch
     a man get dressed.
Some place where box turtles
     sun themselves on a log.
Some place where they hear
     geese fly overhead.
Some place where their breathing matters.

My corner of the morning sky—
where am I supposed to live?

EARLY SUNDAY MORNING – WAITING

Crossing the Rio Grande, Dad –
driving west.
This is Indian country – vast,
stark, dry land dotted
with juniper bushes and piñon trees
that hug the ground.

Sandia mountain range feels
heat touch its shoulders.
It is late spring; today our sun rises
on the mountain's northern–most peak.

Someone honors the bones –
placing skulls on dirt mounds,
dead tree limbs inside
circles of stones. Flutes play, and
I pray silently, deeply –
"Bring us another rain, God."

I close my eyes and wait
with the mountains
for cooling, soothing rain
to touch our shoulders.

IN LOVE WITH MORNING

I am so in love with morning
shadows cast on my patio.
The bold strut of pigeons
move with caution across the yard
to avoid my primal howl.

The musical hum of motorcars
a block away, serenade the peace
hanging out on the patio.
A cup of coffee sits with me
sharing a beat up table
wounded by who knows what.

The weeds rejoice over
last night's rain, know their time
is short before the pulling ritual begins.
I am happy just sitting,
no guilt surrounds this space.

Words dance in my head
with no obvious destination.
Today is a writing day
and my pen storms the blank page.

ACCEPTANCE

He walks in the vineyard
contemplating life.
Love tears stream down his face,
soothe the pain of many lifetimes.

A battered soul comes to the place
where the land is ripe for harvest.
He feels ready to receive the gift
of Divine Love resting in the soil.

He has been here before
and turned his face from the light,
doubt, fear and vanity
always his hold cards.

Today, naked and seasoned with experience,
he opens his arms and says,
Master please accept me
as a soldier in your army
to save humanity.

A vine slowly rises from the earth,
encircles his heels.

HALL OF MEMORY

In the hall of my memory bank,
there are images of our youth
floating on maple leaves.

Each colorful entry
floats in ruby red, dusty rose,
amber sunshine, pumpkin orange,

or maple sugar brown.
Some nestle in chocolate on the ground.
Each leaf has a tale

of the sweets of love,
safely residing in the hall.
Only you may unlock the door

to look inside,
the place we share
with memories close to our hearts.

Helping Hands

A group member reaches out
to touch your hand.
A pulling back and bowed head
signals a soul hesitant to face
the fear of flesh that holds one
back from the loving embrace
of helping hands.

Members move forward,
tell their stories of gain and loss.
Each epic battle a challenge,
an opportunity realized
as one inch of flesh
dissipates with each battle won.

Hands reach out to embrace your struggle
until the day arrives,
you surrender to the blessing
of friendship sitting with you.

You focus on your goal
and the weight disappears.
You graduate from fear
knowing the support of others
is always with you
with an outstretched hand.

BRIDE MOON

The robins are singing the full moon down
on this cool April morning.

The Bride Moon, all in white,
walks the aisle of the westward sky
      her path strewn with the petals
      of bird song and stars

As all brides do,
she outglows her handmaidens,
named Planets and Stars.

Slowly, regally,
to a march heard only
in her heart
      she processions toward her Horizon Groom.

BLACK MAGIC WOMAN

Jamaican, she is –
the night sky:

a large, beautiful, dark–skinned woman.

Her back to us,
skirts adrape,
sensuous, sensitive feet asplay
in R.C. Gorman repose

Proud head high,
thick with matted Rastafarian plaits pinned up
with shining planets
      themselves stomping in dancing rhythm
      to her aliveness.

Night Sky Mother –
      rounded shoulders
      dimpled spine
      cradle arms perpetual in lullaby,
gathering unto her the blackest
of black holes,
the waywardest
of wandering galaxies.
Soothingly she moans,
hushedly –
her very breathing
      the song itself.

So dark she is, so
expansive,
So soft her curves,
she takes her invisibility for granted.

Ah,
but there's the sickle moon
rippling from her left scapula as
she's rocking, rocking ...
There
the starlight pinpoints of her
lushly, wondrously tattooed body.

And there, at dawn,
the gemstone sun –
the open wound
       of her heart in
       its saffron radiance.

YOGA

Marion's house
has the
biggest crickets I ever saw.
This morning at 6:00 a.m.
I corralled one in a Kleenex.
It escaped the fate of the flush,
as out the back door we went
to freedom and life.

The moon!
Startling, full, Eucharistic
in the western horizon,
<u>being</u> the western horizon.
That black cricket leaped so far,
the white moon has a black spot.

You can't see it, though.
There's a
dainty doily cloud
floating like drapery
over Black Cricket's new home.

Marion's house
has the
biggest crickets I ever saw.

PHONE CALL

On an impulse
I picked up the phone
and called you.

The act wasn't so
weighty as
choosing a fork in
the road, but still

a dead end

FEBRUARY PROMISE OR LACK THEREOF

On this February winter's day
When spring lies only weeks away
I start to resent the weary cold
And tire of the dreary gray
Of mornings that unfold
With dawn of rose and gold
Then belie their early promise and replay
The same old song with which they went away

But though I know lengthening days soon will turn
Willows and early plants to green
I have an ancient fear I can't unlearn
That rites must always show we mean
To honor all the gods of spring
So they will grace the world with their return.

ABOUT SAND, A TRIOLET

Wind likes to play with sand
Building waves or stacking up a dune
Or leveling furrows plowed up in the land.
Wind likes to play with sand.
Wind throws it up roiling grand
Clouds that block out the sun at noon.
Wind likes to play with sand
Building waves or stacking up a dune.

HOW BAGELS GOT TO NEW MEXICO, AND ENCHILADAS GOT TO PHILADELPHIA

When we go away we take
More than us along
Even though we should be quite enough.

Instead our beliefs go along for the ride.
What we know tints what we see.
What we believe filters what we take in.
What we prefer dictates our perception.
So where we go cannot be complete
Until we change it to what we came from.

We don't become where we are
We make where we are become where we were
No matter where you go there you are
Sounds dumb but is really profound
Look around you wherever you are.
If you aren't there, then you will make it
So that you are.

I Cherish a Good Resentment

I have some good resentments that I cherish.
They are so rich I will not let them perish.
Any time I want I can call them to my mind
And massage them and twist them as I try to find
A perfect act of vengeance I might commit
To allay the resentments that on my heart still sit.
But I must be careful that I don't release
So many that I might have to cease
Plotting and turning them in my brain
Because they really don't cause me that much pain.
They are actually such a source of pleasure
So I will keep a good supply to treasure.

BLUE HYDRANGEAS

Blue hydrangeas
In a blue pot
On a table,
Dressed in green.

Clustered blossoms
Like raindrops dry
They shrivel, then
Resurrect with water.

Blue like sky
Azure like prayer
A friend's gift.

Reunion

We gather under Cottonwoods
on a warm night
anticipation tickling the air.
Everyone looks familiar,
just further down the road.
Some still sport longish hair,
others not much hair at all.
Mini–skirts and no bras have morphed into
sensible shoes and oversize T–shirts to
hide the bulges –– lots of bulges.
Canes, walkers and wheelchairs have become as
common as LSD tabs. The energy is the same though –
loving, friendly, happy, even though the decade we remember
has become our age.
Wild applause as he crosses the stage –
hat, sunglasses and long, white hair familiar.
The cane he uses, new.
He reaches the piano and the first notes
transport us back to youth. His voice plays
with us, teases us, encourages us to remember.
Soon we are laughing, screaming, dancing
on our feet, in our chairs – we dance as our old bodies
give way to the common memory.
The moon rises above the trees as the evening ends and
we rise to go, smiling at each other and shaking our heads.
A connection has been resurrected. We are a tribe.
We are a family.

PREDATOR

He walks into the dark bar and stands,
letting his eyes adjust.
His nostrils expand as he registers the scent of
stale beer, dust and boredom.
He scans the room and then heads
toward the bar where she sits alone
with her drink.
He assesses her as he approaches –
fading beauty, too much makeup,
weight slipping up behind.
He sits close to her, orders a drink,
shows his teeth and says,
"Hey delicious, can I buy you a drink?"

I SHALL EAT STRAWBERRIES

I have longed for them
from childhood when I learned
their kiss could be fatal.
Their color neon in the market,
no other color matches it.
The promise of juice
flooding mouth, dribbling back through
lips , caressing throat. The slight
crunch of soft pulp. I can
feel it in my dreams.

I have lived a lifetime and
through times good and bad,
they have been a presence –
something to fear, a promise of peace.
Now I am old. People I loved and
lived with – all gone.
Body failing and the violence of
this era, an assault every day.
I look at strawberries with a
new understanding. I take them from
the refrigerator, roll one in my hand,
feel the weight of
its hidden treasure.

Before I die, I will feel
their flesh surrender to my teeth.
Before my tongue swells, I will
explore fully the luxury of their
flavor. Before my throat closes,
some of the juice will
seep down, satisfying a thirst
that has lasted decades
I shall be found with
sticky, red lips, the hint of
a smile on my face and
I shall smell of strawberries.

A WINTER'S WAKE: SONG FOR THE SOLSTICE

Now is the turn to light, night letting go
its coldest hold on the folds of dark December.
The longest night stretches out the shadows
feeling along the lengthening of its way
toward the day of the prodigal sun's return.

Light gains from the wane of the dark
eyes of ice, the cold fires of star–flakes
sparked from the bristling fur of night.
Dusk is turning inside out
waxing in measures of moon.

Out of the mouth of night
warm breath spins the white web
of the planet's branching,
springs to wake
the years new–found hours.

Walking the Bosque

It's June, Russian olive
in bloom,
little scented
yellow stars
surrounded by sharp
thorns.
How do the birds
who eat their olives
avoid the thorns?

Along the acequia
the water wrinkles
as I begin to think.

I'd like to match
what happens to me
with what I need

when I trip over
a cottonwood root.

"Come back, my psyche cries.
Come back to this moment
this now, this here"

where the air hangs lightly

in the sun's rays,
where under my feet
weeds grow
so intricate
as to make me pause
in wonder.

KEEPING THE PROMISE

The last day of August
the beginning—almost—
of autumn, season of chrysanthemums
already September light slants forward

We'll need the warmth of fall leaves
their brightening colors of fire
to hold us through the long bitter winter.

What's left of autumn in November
are ghosts, expectations, memories,
promises, visions

Visions
of summer, summer's repetition
of green becomes more faint
as darkness descends ever earlier.

We need to know that leaves
will grow again with light,
what we cling to as these leaves
scatter at our feet, their clinging
over for now.

A Found Poem from My Journal

Peace roses fade
in the twilight, the limbs
of the cottonwood seem
to lift to frame Venus
rising to the west.

The sleeping beasts
of the mountains huddle together
while clipper ships of cloud
in the sea of sky sail away
toward the dark curve
of the horizon. In the last light
before the first star guides them
into night, they'll take me with them
just for looking.

SUNDAY LATE

Sunday late,

Winds are restless,

Clouds, heavy and blue,

Mountains rise with sunset,

Crags of shadow fill my eyes,

And I still have laundry to do.

ALBUQUERQUE AUTUMN

Blue sky,
Awash in light.
Black highways
Gleam like shores.

Overpasses fly,
Gull wings.
Train tracks,
Whitecaps.

Buildings squat
Like sunbathers.
People meander
Like crabs.

Tall glass buildings,
Like tall ships,
Sail color;
Trees splash, yards drift.

The tide turns;
A cool swell.
East, Watermelon high.
West, crimson veil.

Eve, Night's bosom,
Heaven's children.
Luminous valley,
Sleeping Beauty.

The Moon
Slips to bed.
The stars
Cast dreams.

SILENT DIN

I sat
In church.
She stood
Before me.

Her figure
Flowed
Like a
Waterfall.

Her earth
Danced
Beneath
The eddies.

My heart
Fell in.
Rapids.
Silent din.

Her beauty,
Tsunami.
Debacle
Beat me.

When Beauty
Says hello,
I turn to
Dust.

I sat
In church.
The sermon,
Lust.

FALLING IN LOVE

Falling in love

Is your first music lesson.

FALLING STAR

a falling star streaks the night

how many eyes have caught its flight
how many hearts
have skipped a beat at that sight
how many souls have wished and wished
and in that wishing moment felt delight
and briefly forgot their daily plight

inhale the essence of that star
taste it
roll it around on your tongue
savor it
swallow it
then   deep inside
revel in the magic of your wish

THE LOAN OF LOVE

mutual love   has no need of
a receiver and a sender
there's nothing to own
just a precious loan
to be returned to the lender

for as love travels back and forth
in mutual adoration
in strength it grows
as passion flows
from amorous reciprocation

so do not hoard this love I lend
embrace it in ecstasy
let it enthrall
but please don't stall
to lend it back to me

THE LOST WORD

sometimes when speaking with my peers
the word I need next disappears

I pause and probe   what was that word
I know I know it   it's absurd
I knew that word a moment back
but now my talking's off the track

it starts with an "s" or is it a "t"
or maybe an "m" or perhaps a "p"

a slew of words now flood my brain
they just don't fit   don't mean the same

and so my friends just stand and stare
that word I needed   it just ain't there

then maybe in an hour or three
that wayward word wends back to me

against that word I raise cry and hue
"Where were you when I needed you?"

BEN AND ME

one of the things that's puzzling to me
is that who I am is not whom I see

I look in the mirror the face that I see
looks quite familiar but it's not really me

you look at my face call me Ben that's my name
but my name and me we're just not the same

my name's but a veil behind which I hide
the only true me is the one that's inside

and everybody I meet just their body I see
'cause 'tween body and brain there's disparity

my body is but an enveloping shroud
to know the real me no one is allowed

the whole world it seems is split in two spheres
the one that we live in the other 'tween ears

I'm that stream of thought that starts when I waken
and flows without pause 'til I'm by sleep overtaken

we humans have come to this unique place
where our self–awareness defines the human race

APRIL'S ESCORT

april awakens knowing
she must chaperon
spring's gust–freighted winds
en route to blind dates
with perinatal leaves
too small to rustle a cry
against the trespass

Bananas Don't Ski

Why must I tear off one banana
from each of a half dozen separate bunches
every time I shop a produce section?
Isn't there some corporate giant like Chiquita
that has sufficient research facilities
to cultivate banana plants where each bunch
has just one banana ripening every day of the week?

The back of my neck wouldn't have to host
condemning eyes of stock boys and fellow shoppers
as I rip off just one banana from each bundle.
Of course if I ever married again   I might prefer
to buy a bunch where two bananas ripen each day.

And what about all those single bananas found alone
scattered among otherwise neatly arranged bunches?
You know for sure those losers have been eagle–eyed
and rejected multiple times when earlier buyers
chose their sibling bunch–mates instead.

I asked the check–out lady, "Why? Why? Why?
She didn't seem to share my concern
and would only say that she freezes ones
that get too ripe and makes banana creamed
                              ...something–or–another.
I said that I thought bananas didn't like the cold
but probably only because they never learned to ski.
And that's too bad because they'd be naturals.

They wouldn't even have to buy skis or boots
just flop over on their backs and swoosh—
off they'd go. If they crashed—no bones to break
                          —no tendons to tear
                —no hyper–chilled digits
          to defrost on face–tingling northwinded days.

And can you imagine a snow covered chalet
hot and cold beverages at an apres–ski party
split oak or white birch ablaze in a stone fireplace
banana ski–bums and banana ski–bunnies   casting
come–hither glances across a chinked–log room
saying, "Peel me baby, peel me."

BURNING RATTLES

mocking river's riffle   a side–winder cuts ripples
    into high desert bosque soil   teasing river
to taste parch beyond its own serpentine curb
    where a hostage has hidden meager supplies
not likely to be missed
    but needed for her escape

she craves being with her lover and no longer
    enslaved to this enemy tribe
no longer taunted as Daughter of Hissing Snake
    nor trapped in a hostile camp during a harsh
season when coyote stole winter's wife
    enraging a relentless storm

under cover of bitten moon and howling wind
    she steals white pony from her captor's village
flees to foothill migration trails of elk and antelope
    then beyond into a bitter high mountain storm
where even strong and persistent braves
    find conditions too perilous for chase

she dreams her passion   too long suppressed
    within her coiled readiness to strike
she envisions freedom tethered to love
    that survives torment and she begs powerful
spirits of all rivers and tall grasses to carry
    her home and to carry time back to their firsts
        the first time their eyes locked
        the first time he touched her cheek
        the first time they knew their passion

and now   now to fix time firmly on those firsts
    at least until her limbs freeze stiff as the tree
until her tears become river he swims
    until her hair returns as tall grass he walks
these are the burning rattles she carries
    still coiled in hope   she holds them still

still   I can feel her cling

PRISONERS OF CIRCUMSTANCE

fog enshrouded vessels moor
wait to wharf
crane to unload freight
refill holds for departure   as

alcatraz sits docked in history
on its nearby island nest
prisoners long departed

embarcadaro summer eve
medicare–elegible lovers
ghirardelli square
chocolate and caffeine nations
favorite cafe   open–air table
night sky's obsidian dome

charming wharf–side details
shy into periphery
eyes softly tether
anchor warm currents
unlaundered emotions
strung between
like flannels basking
on backyard clothesline

one hour before returning
to distant points
separation inevitable
until perhaps
another season's weekend

at this shrine to embarkation
not understanding why
a reach for a tear on a cheek
is the only crane left
refilling our hold
for departure   as

alcatraz sits locked in history
watching us prisoners
of circumstance depart

CUBERO

Red dust sifting under the door
hot dry wind

White and black kitchen tiles
rasp of grit shifting under foot--

Sunlight explodes off a tin roof
a trailer exposed to the glaring skies--

Shadows of a cottonwood drifting
over a one room post office,

Freshly painted white,
beneath a red, blue and white flag

CARDBOARD MAN

He stood erect
stepped neat
swift
back, forth
side to side
slide slide
connecting with the earth light–ly
his feet tapped out
a tidy pattern
pre–cise–ly

An English lady raised in the elegant arts
wedded the handsome profile
the graceful limbs
the dazzling Fred Astaire feet

Because he was the only American she had ever met
who could dance

Because their offspring would be winning

The flirtatious foxtrot and the wistful waltz
spun away the time and she paid
for what she got
as they twirled round and round the seasons
as she offered up her lonesome heart
piece by piece
step by step, beat by beat
to the handsome face

while the tic toc of the valentine heart
kept time
with the dazzling Fred Astaire feet
And their children were good looking

WATER MOVES US FORWARD:
THE CHILDREN MUST BE FED

her breast a white mushroom
blooms improbable round and fertile
on this thirsty scratch of land

things are what they are here here wind flays the world
a capricious god picks things up, smashes them down
grinds them up in its great mortar   the pestle whirls
and whirls and pounds

peas shrivel in pods and corn hardens in husks
and all lie down
before the driving wind

there is pain
grit fills the eye, penetrates intimate crevices, lacerates skin
dust mounds on tongues, in nostrils, ear canals

water moves us forward the children must be fed

the babe's head lolls against the lush
supple squeeze of food
satiated for a moment or awhile
a sweet face gone to blue and green dreams

sleep settles, nestles
against a body of bone and leather
encircled by arms of weathered wood.

Mother
hums a toneless tune
drums the rain
thrums to the will of the earth repeated

water moves us forward, the children must be fed

(Note: This poem was inspired by a photograph titled, "Migrant Mother2," by Dorothea Lange, 1936)

Sox, or I Don't Know How Those Clowns Got into my Poem

I shouldn't mention them, but there they are

Clearly, they don't mate for life, instead renege
and run away with any old clinging thing
like a pair of old mismatched hippies or their slippers
they're totally unprejudiced
will pick a partner of any cloth color or size

no, they want freedom and free love – all that stuff
marriages are arranged at Sox Are Us, but
divorce is instantaneous
the unbinding is unbounded
they were born to confound it: LIFE that is

endlessly bursting out of drawers
like odious red and yellow clowns piling out
of a little clown car
trumpeting for attention, galloping around the house
and then
a quick nap behind the couch

and just when you think there can't possibly be another
there is one more
lurking in a corner of the panty drawer

but now they're all piled upon the floor
like a heap of belligerent toddlers

determined to weed out the loners you discover
that the dull miserly threadbare have a pair
while the lush fancy ones
are on a cruise in the Caribbean

ahhh, so many things can be controlled with guilt and fear
but then
there are sox

OLD–MAN–WINTER

Breath becomes a mist as you speak
Ice forms on a slow moving creek
Leaves fall to the ground
As winter wind twirls them around
Women knit warm wooly shawls
While men bundle–up in snug tight thermals
Life eagerly transforms to a seasonal bliss
Arctic colors change as winter metamorphoses
Snow graces the frozen ground
With white enchantment abound
Shovels emerge to stubborn minds
For winter is not always loved in kind
However, winter helps Nature sleep
As her children harvest crops to reap
The cycle animates in all beasts
Bears hibernate and men make feasts
We celebrate in winter jamboree
Halloween, Thanksgiving, and Christmas glee
This is our time to share love and gratitude
As Old–Man–Winter is considered a beatitude

HOME DELIVERY

Home Delivery
The night was long and exhausting,
but the fate a glorious and blessed one.
On Friday, November fourteenth
in the year of twenty-fourteen,
a new life had just begun.
It was sun rise—the first light of day,
At 5:48 a.m.,
christened Amarissa Lucena.
She weighed in at
six and three-quarter pounds,
with a length of twenty and
three-quarter inches.
A poetic beauty like her mother,
so gentle and precious
as any angel could genuinely be.
I was invited to participate
as a Reiki Practitioner
in the natural birth
in a pool of warm water
in the middle of a living room
in the family's rural home.
An honor it is to uphold
with gratitude and love;
like a Fairy-Godmother
in tribute to a new life.
Forever in reverence,
I shall always be
to her mother and father,

Jasmine and Jose, sincerely,
to have been an active observer
in the miraculous animation
to the birth of an angelic soul.

A PIT MOMENT

I had a pit moment today
where my thought was not clear.
Yesterday, I knew this thought
with clarity, precision and thoughtfulness,
but now, I have lost that thought.
It has left my mind.
I ponder, I daydream
and I thump my head,
but the pit moment lingers;
and my thought is still dead.
Today, which is another day,
I remember that pit moment from yesterday.
I remember the thought that became missing
from my mind. Where it became an abstract moment.
Stranger still, today, I remember it—the thought
with clarity, precision and thoughtfulness.
I do believe
society calls these pit moments:
-Senior Moments
-Brain Freezes
-Brain Farts
whatever they are called
I get them periodically.
Sometimes they arrive
in the most embarrassing element,
and I try to cover the moment up.
This pit moment is not a
savoir-faire, where I feel
I am doing a righteous thing.

Oh no, this lost moment in time
becomes a bewildered paramount
that heralds my senility.
I continue to function
as a normal individual
(well, as normal as one can be)
on my daily routine,
knowing another pit moment
will surely happen again to me;
but maybe, next time, hopefully,
I will be able to cover it up, obscurely.

OIL SPILL: A TRAGEDY

Once pure under Neptune's realm
Oceans clear with life in abundance
A wondrous frontier of coral reefs
And foamy seas with creatures from the deep
Waves high for surfers delight
Where one could play upon its beach
To swim, sail, or cruise without fright
But industry created amuck
With oil and petroleum
As we become horror–struck
Yet, commerce a monetary demon
Controlled by high–society
Impresses upon us with their greed
And we crave the black gold poison
For personal use, and yet, we find—
that we cannot live without it
We heat our homes, we drive our cars
Selfish and needy we have become
There are many who want to make a change
To live by Mother Nature's rule
For if we destroy her beauty
And loose the basics of life
Then our future is forlorn
And forever destroyed for posterity
All earth's inhabitants will endlessly morn
However, there is hope for us yet
Hope for our children's children
For a tragedy can be amended
With hard work, persistence
And whole–hearted determination
It is not too late to change our fate

SUR UN FIL

Funambulist, you are poised
as you flit from building to building
stories above city streets.
You wear a bouncy tutu
trimmed in black lace,
tights, and sensible low-heeled shoes
that do not slip as they make contact with the wire.
In your right hand is an umbrella,
the only thing that wobbles as you dart forward
sur un fil.

Deftly, you keep your center of mass
over the wire
with no safety net.
You have trained for years
using mechanics to develop this routine.
An audience cranes its neck below,
waiting for you to style.

Why are you scurrying so swiftly
along tensioned metal wire
like a squirrel sailing
along telephone lines?
Are you heading
for the bedroom window of a lover
who will salute your unorthodox entry
and gather you up in his arms?

MY MOTHER HANGS IN MY CLOSET

Funny,
how things you give to others
come back to you.
Like the silver–framed picture
of Frida Kahlo
that returned to me
when my friend downsized.
And my mother's red jacket
that hangs in my closet.

My mother who just died
at age 96
loved color—
in paint on walls,
in clothes.
In the '50's she bought
jodhpurs and matching jacket in rose.
My father loudly refused
to take her to a company party
in that outfit.
She stayed home.

Long afterward
I bought her
a red jacket
with multicolored
decorative threads
hanging down jauntily.
She wore it constantly;
it became an old friend.

After she died
I reclaimed the jacket
and took it to the cleaners.
Now it sits in my closet
under a cellophane sheath.
Funny,
how things you give to others
come back to you.

MY MOTHER'S BROTHER

He prayed at the synagogue
each morning, davening in his white
yarmulke and tallit.
He and I performed the unveiling service
at my father's grave site,
reciting the prayers in Hebrew and English.
I took the part of the rabbi; he the cantor.
I took care not to plant
my feet directly on the frozen grave;
he stood on the grave site without hesitation.
At the close of the service a monument in granite
was unsheathed.

It was not his work that made him smile
but the pirouettes he played on the clarinet
that he meticulously cleaned and shined.
He produced a sound molasses–thick
as he blew on the horn that reverberated
through his small house.
He marched in the Redskins Band,
and was a regular with a local
Dixieland combo.

He was buried at the beginning
of the blizzard of the century,
the rabbi chanting the "El Maleh Rachamim,"
the prayer for the departed
who are holy and pure of heart.
The snow spilled down from above,
blanketing the grave site and
family praying in chairs under a white tent,
camouflaged in the whirling snow.

EPHEMERAL

As ephemeral as one more pink hollyhock
that emerges miraculously each morning,
as ephemeral as the new blooms
dangling from the desert willow,
as ephemeral as the red–laced budding
of the bird of paradise,
as ephemeral as the whimsical purple bloom
on the red smoke tree,
as ephemeral as the orange butterfly
quiescent for seconds on the billowing
lavender ground cover,
as ephemeral as the pair of orioles
in yellow and orange
that visited for an evening
and never reappeared—
after I bought them a feeder,
as ephemeral as the greening of
my postage stamp front lawn
in the third year of drought.

NIGHT AT THE BOSQUE

a mostly full moon
winks over the dried stubble in the field
catches a coyote slinking along
pretending he has somewhere to be

two tundra swan
sail noiselessly among the reeds
their long necks curved toward each other
performing some nocturnal pas de deux

it is long past closing time now

a Sandhill crane stands solitary
one leg tucked upward
listening for the sound of the moon

BUTTERFLY

who, what, am I
whence came I
and, really, why

the answers are
not out there
no sudden insights
not here, not now

it is a long, long
journey to the knowing
through the terrible wind
and the faint heat
of the setting sun

but that is
only a façade
it is the looking
on the outside

sometimes, not often,
I am a bird
resting, dancing on
the high wire

that absolute sureness
of being at home
in the sky
with no net below

sometimes, not often,
I am a Monarch butterfly
traveling with my kind
to a place of regeneration

sometimes, not often,
I am a Monarch butterfly
one of thousands with
whom creation begins again

A SHORT SEASON

spring,
the season of
rising expectations

towns bracing
for floods

blooming bulbs pushing
through chilly ground

ladders going up
to retouch winter's spleen

spring,
the season of
rising expectations

but still, I wait
for balmy autumn

golden days
when the sky hovers
lapis blue

that lull
when time is
almost still

and I am
almost certain
I will live forever

easy to imagine
during that small
run of balmy days

DAUGHTER

your hands flared pale
under the moon
shaping an ivory bowl
to hold the night

HOW ODD

to think of never being kissed
like that again
a man who loves a woman
kind of kiss
I want to make love
kind of kiss
a tongue over teeth
tiny bites
on the lips
kind of kiss
a hands behind the neck
hip to hip
nose to nose
kind of kiss
how odd
never again

will I ever not miss it

THE ORANGE CLOUDS IN A SANDIA SUNSET ARE CITRUS–SCENTED

I drink in the juice of the evening colors
Feel the stringent bite on my eyes
Long to squeeze the cloud over homemade vanilla ice cream
The small cuts on my gardener's fingers sting
As I reach toward the sky
Lemon
Lime
Orange
Zest for life explodes above the darkening city
Slowly shrinking up to pinpoints in the black sky
The orchard dies till day

IN THE TIME IT TOOK TO BECOME
A PEBBLE...

a raindrop became a river
a child became a distant ancestor
an acorn was eaten
rejected
became a tree
a table
an ancient artifact

a grunt became a word
a "no" to emerge from
every child's mouth
a phrase to love
became a poem

a stick figure on rocks
became a woven work of art
from imperfect attempts
a chipped piece of obsidian
became a wooly mammoth killer
a small cylinder became a killer of men

AS A CHILD

As a child there was only the thing
      The squishy wiggly prickly hot cold
         bumpy smooth crisp
      The red black green lilac umber
      The loud soft high low drill drone
      The pungent earthy skunky fresh burned sweet
      The salty spicy rancid drippy slimy crunchy

No names to coat the thing with
an incomprehensible aura of importance or permanence

The ancient ones revert to senses to know their world
Names are the first to disappear in the childhood
of our twilight years

A Child is Ever a Child of Mine
(for Michael Dennis)

A child is ever a child of mine
Deserving of love
Deserving of peace.
Memories are constant and enduring
Of a tousled towhead
Or of a freckled–cheek smile.

A child is ever a child of mine
Wish this child rest, that he might
Lay down his earthly burdens
On his journey toward the light.

A child is ever a child of mine
Pray for his continued well–being
And wholeness.
Pray for closure, in time
And for my own wounded soul.

A child is ever a child of mine
And goodbyes are always bittersweet.
Love knows no time or boundaries.
A connection endures.

A child is ever a child of mine.

OJO CALIENTE

Head rests on a rock cove
As tepid water flows from earthen pottery jar
Spilling over ears,
Crown, neck, and shoulders.
Buoyant fingers
Touch slick, slate tiles
In the arsenic pool.
Toes float, yet
Are grounded
To the bottom of the pool.
Voice of water trickles
Playfully in the crevices.
Steam rises slowly
Across the water's surface.
Flow of freedom becomes
Bliss in the moment.
Calming essence
Soothes and settles
Raw nerves, tight muscles,
And aching bones.
At 102 degrees.

Sun illumines cliff walls
With flame-colored light.
A pair of dark ravens
Soar over pools in tandem.

In this special place,
Ecstasy whispers.

BETWEEN THE SPACES

Composing on computer keyboard
Stop....

Look at the spaces between the letters.
Look at spaces between the words.
Look up from the screen,
See blinds meant to shut out sunlight

Look at space between the blinds.
See a pine tree providing shade and supporting
Twine and twig baskets for nesting birds.

Look in the space between the branches.
See a grey, clouded sky.
Look past the clouds and see

A blue clearing.
Look past the blue.
I see the blue of your eyes.

Can you look at me, without doing a "quick scan?"
Seeing just enough to make a snap judgment
Of what is "of value to you" just now.

Do you see the depth of my character?
Do you recognize the good in my soul?
Do you know that there are scattered stars in my pocket?

LIFETHREADS

Guiding,
Steadying,
A gentle nudge this way...or that.

Your large hands
Secure around mine
Clutching the stick
Inserted into an unraveling ball of twine.

You anchor the kite strings.
You ground me.
You shelter me from being
Ferried aloft
By wayward gusts.

You, likewise, tether me
Through life's gale storms.
You are always smiling
At my progress.

Your hands are my harbor,
My lifethreads.

CONTRIBUTOR BIOGRAPHIES

Olga Anson is a native of the Land of Enchantment with roots in northern New Mexico. As a graduate of the University of New Mexico, her professional career led her to develop and direct educational, social service and occupational programs for State and Federal governments in New Mexico, Nevada, California and Colorado. She began writing poetry in her teens. Her creative spirit was further inspired with awe for the natural world after travel to New Zealand, France, and Germany. She combines music with her poetry and is also an avid singer and songwriter.

Clara Ann Bowler is a retired lawyer. She was educated at the University of Chicago and DePaul University. She published poetry in and helped edit an early feminist literary magazine titled *Primavera*. She is an avid gardener and receives poetic inspiration from her backyard flower garden.

Trish Claflin was born in Ohio and lived in Florida for forty years before coming to live in New Mexico in 1992. She graduated from the University of Florida in 1953 with a degree in anthropology. She is a member of Phi Beta Kappa, an honorary scholastic society. Her poetry is influenced by her appreciation of nature and wildlife.

Donald DeNoon is a native of Indiana. He made career stops in Kentucky, Maryland, Missouri and Nevada before arriving in Albuquerque 26 years ago. A retired minister and counselor, he started writing poetry in sixth grade, continued off and on, but didn't get serious about writing until moving to New Mexico. His poems have appeared in numerous anthologies and local publications.

Deborah Barba Eagan has a love of nature that is reflected in her poems. She learned Spanish as a child and is from a bilingual family in Las Cruces, New Mexico. She sprinkles Spanish throughout many of her poems. As the Albuquerque Tricentennial Poet in 2006, her poem titled "Come See Albuquerque" was published.

Jeanne Favret was raised in Columbus, Ohio. She moved to New Mexico in 2004 for the beauty of the light and the landscape. Her poems have been published in *Recently Eclipsed*, *The Rag*, *Central Avenue*, *Adobe Walls*, *Turtle Music*, and *Medical Muse*. She has been a member of the New Mexico Poetry Alliance since 2005.

Teresa E. Gallion has published in numerous journals and anthologies. She has a chapbook, *Walking Sacred Ground*, a CD, *On the Wings of the Wind* and two books, *Contemplation in the High Desert* and *Chasing Light*. You may preview her work at the websites noted below: http://bit.ly/1aIVPNq and http://bit.ly/13IMLGh

Elizabeth Hurst Waitz enjoyed writing poems as a child. As a certified court reporter (stenographer) since 1985, she's listened to and transcribed other people's words a lot more than she's written down her own. With deep admiration for Hafiz for his spiritual wisdom, Garrison Keillor for his people wisdom, and Mary Oliver for her nature wisdom, Elizabeth has an expanding sense of wonder and appreciation for all mysteries of the written word yet to be revealed.

Karen McKinnon has had poetry appear in numerous magazines and anthologies, including the University of New Mexico Press anthology, In Company: An Anthology of New

Mexico Poets After 1960. Her memoir in prose and poetry, Set in Motion, was published by The Wildflower Press. She teaches poetry writing through the University of New Mexico's Osher Lifelong Learning Institute.

Jack Markham has been writing poetry for more than 60 years. He was born in Wheeler, Texas and grew up in northeastern New Mexico and the northwest Texas Panhandle. In 1963, he moved to Gallup, New Mexico and taught high school English. He then went to graduate school at the University of New Mexico. He was an assistant principal then the principal of Farmington High School. He spent his last six years in education as a junior high school teacher. Jack and his wife, Evelyn, moved to Albuquerque to be near aging parents. They have two grown sons and two great daughters–in–law.

Kathy Maxson is a retired teacher who has lived in New Mexico more than 30 years. She enjoys reading, writing, lunching, sewing, margaritas, and watching the sun come and go. She has been published locally and in the book, *Illuminations*.

Raymond Mock is an electronic technician by trade and has written poetry since the 1980s. He has published one other poem, "A Smile," in *The Promise of Tomorrow* by The National Library of Poetry in 1997 and again that year by the same publisher in *A Celebration of Poets: Showcase Edition*. Written from heartfelt experience, his poems are fundamentally non–fiction.

Ben Nurry started to write poetry about 18 years ago back in his native state of Pennsylvania. He is particularly fond of rhyming and alliteration. He often revises his poems and considers them forever works in progress.

Marty O'Malley lives in Albuquerque, but originally hails from Minnesota and Wisconsin. He enjoys skiing, poetry, eastern metaphysics, quantum physics, and working sudokus. He has bachelor's degrees in math, physics, and chemistry as well as a master's of business administration, plus CPA and CMA certifications. He has taught collegiate accounting and management classes. In addition to teaching at universities, he was in charge of management consulting for CPA firms, CEO of one healthcare organization and VP–Finance of another before serving on the Presbyterian Medical Group Executive Council and its predecessor boards and committees for 15 years. He likes to meld quantum physics, skiing, and metaphysics into his poetry.

Prudence Page grew up in Chicago. She made her first adult home in Switzerland and remains baffled to this day as to why she returned to Chicago. She was a teacher for many years. In 1994 she moved to New Mexico. She has come to love the Southwest for its beauty and its hospitality to poets and artists of all kinds.

Annmarie Pearson has been writing for more than 20 years. Her work has been published in *Playboy Magazine, Valencia County News–Bulletin, the University of New Mexico Valley Visions,* and the *New Mexico Breeze,* among others. She has published two books: a mystery/detective sleuth novel, *The Fetish Ruby,* and a novelty/ poetry/ photograph book. She lives in Los Lunas, New Mexico.

Bonnie Rucobo was born in Washington, D.C. and raised in Maryland. She attended Northwestern University's Medill School of Journalism and graduated from Reed College in Portland, Oregon. She worked for National Public Radio. She graduated from law school at Golden Gate University in San Francisco. She is published in several anthologies. Her first novel, *King Pachuco and Princess Mirasol*, was published, as well as the sequel. She is a docent at the Albuquerque Museum of Art and History.

Claudine R. Sattler grew up in the Missouri Ozarks. She went to law school at Georgetown and is now a practicing attorney. She came to Albuquerque in 1991 from the Navajo Nation where she lived and worked for seven years. She started writing poetry in the 1970s and has had several of her works published. Her favorite subjects are the Southwest, particle physics, war, Biblical characters, and whatever else catches her fancy.

Joann Sheets is a retired teacher from Albuquerque Public Schools and the University of New Mexico. She grew up in the Adirondack Mountains of northern New York State and moved to New Mexico in 1971. She is an acute observer of people, places, and critters. Her works were included in the *66 Poems from the Route*, a publication of the Fresh Ink of New Mexico poetry group. She was a third-place winner in the National Amateur Poetry Competition and her poem "Was and Where" is included in the anthology titled, *Across the Way*.

Karin Stangl has had her award-winning poetry published in numerous magazines and anthologies including *Crosswinds*, *Willow Street*, *Turtle Music*, and *Adobe Walls*. She lives in Albuquerque and is a public relations consultant. She has bachelor's and master's degrees from the University of New Mexico. Her avocation is writing poetry. She is inspired by nature and her travels. She had a chapbook titled *Cranberry Beads* published in 2006.